DANGEROUS ANIMALS

Edited by Damian Kelleher

Written by Richard Stoneman

A **TWO-CAN** BOOK
published by
THOMSON LEARNING

DANGEROUS ANIMALS

First published in the United States in 1995
by Thomson Learning
115 Fifth Avenue
New York, NY 10003

First published in the UK
in 1994 by Two-Can Publishing Ltd.

Library of Congress Cataloging-in-Publication Data

Stoneman, Richard, 1960-
    Dangerous animals / edited by Damian Kelleher :
written by Richard Stoneman
            p.   cm. -- (Info adventure)
    Includes index.
    ISBN: 1-56847-411-3 (hardcover)
    ISBN: 1-56847-318-4 (pbk.)
    1. Dangerous animals—Juvenile literature.
[1. Dangerous animals.] I. Kelleher, Damian. II.
Title. III. Series.
QL100.S76 1995   94–43523

Printed in Italy

Design by Elizabeth Bell. Art directed by Catherine Page. Picture research by Debbie Dorman. Production by Lis Clegg. Additional research by Amanda Tomlin.

Picture credits:
Oxford Scientific Films: 5tl, 6/7, 7tr, 8, 12cl,br, 13, 14, 16/17, 18bl, 18/19, 19brB, 20bl, 23, 24/25, 25tr,bc, 28;
Planet Earth Pictures: 5r, 11, 20/21, 25cr, 28/29; NHPA: 4, 7br, 9, 19brA, 24tl, 29br; Bruce Coleman Ltd: 12tr, 15;
Mary Evans: 22, 27br; Animal Photography: 26; Metropolitan Police: 26/27; DJ Dorman: 27tr.

Illustrations:
Chris West: 4br, 7, 9, 12, 15, 22, 30/31; Phil Gascoine: 4l; Woody: 5; Oliver Frey: 10/11, 22/23.

CONTENTS

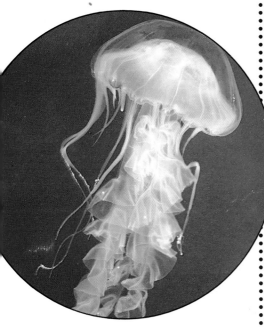

DANGER! DANGER!

Not all animals are as cuddly as pussycats. Some can be petrifying!

▲ *Coming face to face with Cerberus was hell for the ancient Greeks!*

When was the last time you were scared silly by an animal?

Maybe you watched a frightening film about a shark that was terrorizing a sleepy seaside town? Or a movie about a man-eating crocodile? Or perhaps you just came across a spider in the bath!

Most of us fear animals that we will probably never come into contact with in the course of our everyday lives. But just turn on the TV or take a trip to the movies and there they are –

in amazing technicolor detail, larger than life and twice as frightening.

NATURALLY FRIGHTENING

Animals can be roughly divided into two groups – those that eat plants (*herbivores*) and those that eat meat (*carnivores*).

Killing is a natural instinct for a carnivorous creature, and one that is vital to its survival. A tiger that can't hunt and kill is one that will not survive for long. Animals depend upon other animals as food sources – any imbalance in this "food chain" can have a negative effect on all kinds of creatures.

Since the beginning of time, humans have been fascinated by fables about huge beasts. In Greek mythology Cerberus (above left), the hideous three-headed hound, was watch-dog to the underworld. As if his three heads weren't enough, he had a matching mane of slithery serpents. Pity the poor mailperson!

These days, there are all

sorts of other creatures that strike fear into the hearts of humans. But the one animal that's reputed to be the most aggressive in the world is one you've probably never even heard of – the innocuous-sounding African honey badger, or ratel.

DON'T RATTLE A RATEL

Vicious and quite ruthless, these ferocious fighters use their powerful jaws to crack open the shells of turtles and tortoises. So fearless are ratels that they have been known to walk in a straight line through the middle of a

▲ *Vampire bats have special razor-edged teeth – perfect for making a tiny wound from which they can lap up blood!*

herd of elephants! What's more, they have also set upon humans in brutal attacks. Fortunately, the ratel is a nocturnal prowler in its native Africa and Asia, so unless you're out and about after nightfall, a chance encounter with the belligerent honey badger is a rare event.

In a colder part of the world, polar bears also have a reputation for being hard-

▲ *The honey badger is not as cute as its name suggests!*

▲ *You wouldn't want a bear hug from one of these!*

▲ *The ferocious roar of the tiger keeps its enemies at bay*

hearted, wily hunters. It's true, the polar bear is perfectly camouflaged to sneak up on its prey with remarkable ease, but its strategy is not calculated – it comes as second nature. Survival is their prime motivation and polar bears (some of the largest carnivores in the world) need a colossal amount of food. Anything that moves in a wild Arctic wasteland will look like a potential food source to a polar bear – and that means it's fair game.

POISONOUS PERILS

Some animals seem to have an unfair advantage when it comes to trapping or killing prey or just telling enemies to buzz off. Venomous species such as wasps and cobras inject poison into their chosen victims, using parts of their body which have been specially adapted for the task.

Other poisonous animals must be swallowed before their toxins get to work. The puffer (or porcupine) fish, for example, is best avoided when you're serving chips! A generous helping of this fish can result in numbness, convulsions, and even death. But it's unlikely you'll ever tuck into a puffer. When threatened by predators, it blows itself up into a painful ball of spikes, making it too prickly to touch. Ouch!

AND THE WINNER IS...

So when the chips are down, what is the world's most dangerous animal? The vicious ratel? The terrifying tiger? The great white shark? Or the lethal cobra? In terms of sheer killing power, there's one animal that has finished off more people than World War I and World War II. But it's not the sort of animal that tends to inspire chilling nightmares. Yes, it's the malaria-spreading, blood-sucking mosquito (see page 23)! And you thought vampire bats were scary...

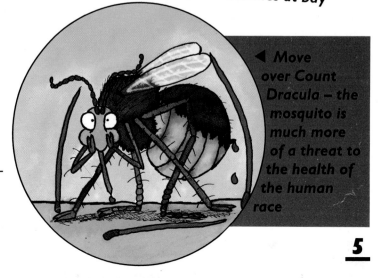

◀ *Move over Count Dracula – the mosquito is much more of a threat to the health of the human race*

5

According to a famous fairy tale, when the princess gave the frog a tender kiss he was transformed into a handsome prince – kerpow! But there's one frog that no princess in her right mind would want to embrace…

It may not look like a killer, but the golden poison arrow frog of western Colombia produces the deadliest poison in the animal world. Just 0.00001 of a gram is enough to kill a single princess, and the average golden poison arrow frog contains enough of the stuff to do away with 1,500 people. That's pretty powerful poison!

DEADLY TIP

There are more than 100 known kinds of poison arrow frogs. These brightly colored beauties are sometimes called arrow poison or poison dart frogs. They were named after some native tribes in tropical America who tip their hunting arrows and blowpipe darts with the deadly poison.

Just before they set off, the tribespeople pin the frogs to the ground with sharp sticks or warm the frogs over an open fire, before rubbing their darts or arrows all over the body of the frog. At the top of each dart there's a small groove where the poison is stored as it dries. Such a dart is effective for a whole year and will quickly paralyze any animals it wounds.

HARD TO SWALLOW

It's difficult to believe, but there are some predators that are capable of swallowing a poison arrow frog – and still live to tell the tale! The frog-eating snake, for example, seems unaffected by the poison and will happily put one away as its dish of the day!

Many other kinds of frogs also produce poison, although it's not quite as toxic as the poison arrow frog. As soon as an animal has a frog in its jaws, the poison on its body will give a burning sensation that causes its potential predator to drop it in dismay. Meanwhile, the frog can hop off to safety!

Sheer dart attack: ▶ poison arrow frogs like this one certainly stand out from the crowd

YOU MUST BE CROAKING!

Did you know this frog has enough poison to kill 1,500 people? Now that's what we call dangerous!

WHAT'S YOUR POISON?

★ It's not just the strength of an animal's poison that determines how dangerous it is. Size is all-important, too!

STONE ME! ▶

When it comes to fish, the one that should always get away is the stonefish – the most poisonous fish in the world. Touch its poisonous spines and you've really cashed in your chips!

◀ SPIDER IN YOUR SHOES

The most venomous spiders are the large Brazilian wandering spiders called phoneutria fera. They wander into people's homes and hide in their clothes and shoes. If disturbed, these nasty nippers give a beastly bite... over and over again.

▲ SCORPION RISING

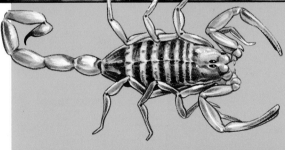

The most venomous scorpion in the world is the Palestine yellow. Fortunately, it only delivers a small amount of poison when it bites, so human deaths are rare.

KILLER KING

The king cobra of Asia is the longest poisonous snake in the world. It grows to nearly 18 feet in length, and one bite from this right royal reptile can kill a small elephant. Luckily for us, they don't seem to pick on humans.

Now turn the page for more snaky statistics!

7

Snakes alive! Did you know there are 270 kinds of snakes which can harm or even kill people with their poison (known as venom)? Poisonous snakes inject venom into the blood of their victims after piercing the skin with sharp, needle-like fangs. The poison is stored inside the fangs, which are hollow. Once you've been bitten, there's no time to waste.

LETHAL INJECTION

Animals that use poisons to attack their victims need to inject the toxin directly into the bloodstream. Even the venom of a rattlesnake is relatively harmless if applied to the skin or swallowed. Imagine this: an adult would need to drink 750,000 times the amount of rattlesnake venom injected in a single bite to achieve the same end result – death!

Rather like toxic spiders (see pages 24-25), snakes are quite shy and will only bite people when disturbed. Most snake bites take place when someone accidentally steps on a snake, so it's normally the foot or lower leg that gets bitten. But once a human has been nipped,

▲ *Ferocious fangs: the red diamondback rattlesnake*

snake bites need urgent attention. There are medicines called *antivenins* which can counteract the effect of a bite.

Antivenins are produced by injecting horses with snake venom. The horses build up a resistance and their blood serum (the fluid that separates from blood when it clots) can then be used to help people recover from bites. But there's no time to waste — snake bites need complicated medical treatment, so the sooner the victim can get to a hospital, the better.

VENOM VICTOR

There's no simple answer to which is the world's most poisonous snake. Much depends on when the snake has last eaten, how recently it has bitten, and, of course, the health of the animal or human it bites. Sea snakes are highly venomous — the species *hydrophis belcheri* is said to possess poison 100 times more toxic than that of the deadly Australian taipan, whose bite can kill a human in a few minutes.

But if you're looking for killer machines, the saw-scaled viper takes some beating. This aggressive, fast-moving, and surprisingly small serpent has a bad reputation — it is responsible for more human deaths than any other snake. The viper is widespread throughout Africa and tends to live in heavily populated areas. What's more, a single adult snake has enough poison to do away with eight adult humans!

SPITTING IMAGE

★ *The black-necked spitting cobra of Africa may not bite – but this snake means business nonetheless! Puffing out its hood to warn of an attack, its trick is to spit painful venom into the eyes of its enemies, which can blind them. Wily field workers in Africa wear shiny badges which act as decoys to distract the snake's aim away from their eyes.*

BITE BACK

Poisonous snakes fall into three types:

A **Back-fanged.** The venom runs down the grooves of these short fangs, which are at the back of the snake's mouth.

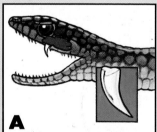

B **Cobras.** The venom flows through their longer, tubular fangs at the front of the mouth.

C **Vipers.** Their long, hollow fangs can be folded away and hidden in fleshy tissue when not in use. When the snake is ready to strike, the fangs are pushed to the front of the mouth by a jaw movement.

Danger, ▶ danger! The taipan is one of the world's deadliest snakes.

9

According to statistics, you're more likely to die from a brush with an elephant than a shark encounter.

KILLER INSTINCT

Meet your ultimate nightmare – a one-and-a-half-ton killing machine straight out of a film set!

There's no doubt about it, films such as *Jaws* have given sharks a reputation as the bad boys of the briny. **But don't write them off before you know the full facts.**

The truth is, sharks are responsible for very few attacks on humans each year – not even as many as 100. That's not much consolation to the victims who do get bitten, however, and with at least five sets of teeth in its mouth at any one time, a shark can certainly bite. Each shark goes through about 20,000 gnashers in its lifetime, with a lost tooth being replaced by a new one which moves forward into its place.

ALL WHITE?
The most dangerous kinds of shark are the great white, the tiger shark, and the bull shark. The great white, inspiration behind *Jaws*, is the largest predatory fish in the world. It grows up to 20 feet long and has razor-sharp teeth as long as a finger.

Despite the impression given by films such as *Jaws*, the most common shark enemy is not ruthless human hunters with grudges, but other, larger sharks. Even baby sharks have to beware of their own parents who may just snap them up for breakfast! Other favorite items on the shark supper menu include turtles, sea birds, seals, and dolphins. A great white will shear its victim into pieces, biting hard and twisting the head and body around. The edges of a great white's teeth

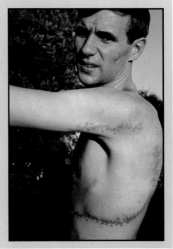

SHORT SHARK SHOCK
▶ *Ouch – that hurt! Shark bite victim Rodney Fox shows off his real-life shark scars*

are serrated to help them saw through huge chunks of flesh in a trice.

KILLER INSTINCTS
In the fine art of hunting, this powerful predator is an old master. Steered by its strong tail, the great white uses its highly sensitive eyes to scan the depths of murky waters, seeking out its next meal. Once the canny killing machine picks up a scent with its super-sharp powers of smell and hearing, the result is a foregone conclusion. Game over.

QUICK QUIZ
★ How many times more powerful than yours are a great white's jaws?

a) 50 times
b) 100 times
c) 300 times

Answer on page 32

There are more dangers of the deep lurking overleaf. Dare you turn the page?!

DANGEROUS WATERS

Sharks aren't the only creepy critters that lurk beneath the waves. These marine monsters are enough to make you want to chuck your swimsuit away for good!

THE STING

★ *The long, whiplike tail of the stingray has one or two sharp spines on its back. They are edged with barbs, and at the base of the spine are poison glands. Step on a stingray and it'll whip up its tail, giving a sting as ghastly as a snakebite.*

CRIKEY IT'S SPIKEY!

When an enemy or intruder scares a puffer (or porcupine) fish, the fish can fill its stomach with water. This makes it puff up like a balloon, causing its sharp spines to stick out. As if that wasn't enough to put you off, this spiky swimmer has another trick up its sleeve – it's poisonous to eat!

WIBBLY, WOBBLY, DEADLY

★ *There's nothing delicious about the jellyfish. It has tentacles with stinging cells which explode when touched, driving tiny, poisonous, paralyzing threads into its victim. The jellyfish then gets to work on phase two: digesting its prey!*

The Portuguese man-of-war can kill a person. But the loggerhead turtle isn't scared – it will happily eat a man-of-war, even though its head gets stung so badly it can hardly see what it's eating.

SHOCKING!

★ *There are about 500 kinds of fish that can generate their own electricity. Best known of the bunch is the electric eel. In three pairs of electric organs, which work like batteries, this slimy shocker can produce 500 volts – enough to knock out a horse.*

GREEDY EATERS!

A shoal of piranhas in a feeding frenzy can strip the flesh from a large animal in minutes. They never stop growing so these famished fish are always hungry. Their small, triangular, needle-sharp teeth come in very handy at meal times (which can be at any time). Piranhas rarely attack people, but in 1981, more than 300 passengers were killed and eaten when an overloaded boat capsized in Brazil.

Hip hip HOOR-AAAARGH!

They look harmless enough but don't be fooled – we're talking Jaws II here!

Harmless hippo? Ha, ha, ha. The hippopotamus is probably responsible for more human deaths in Africa than any other wild beast.

Herds of hippos graze on land by night, eating fruit, grass, leaves, and vegetables. So once the sun goes down, it's time to be on your guard.

SMASH AND GRAB
With their large, curved front teeth and massive 24-inch long, conical canines at the side, the hippo's mouth is filled with some of nature's deadliest weapons. And don't think you can escape by taking to the water – some of the bad-tempered old buffers have been known to smash up small boats on rivers with their powerful jaws. When they return to the water after feeding, they are particularly dangerous and may attack anyone who crosses their path. You have been warned!

▲ The eagle is landing: America's national emblem, the bald eagle

QUICK QUIZ

Which bird of prey did Napoleon choose as a symbol of his empire?

Answer on page 32

◀ Wise guy: owls are silent swoopers who prey by night

What a carrion! The vultures gather ▶

Feathered FIENDS

Who'd be a bird of prey? Just one look at its menu would be enough to put anyone off – reptiles, small mammals, and even other birds! The fact is that birds of prey (or raptors, as they are sometimes called) are ruthless killing machines, flying flesh-eaters that either hunt and kill their own prey or eat decaying animals already slaughtered by someone else. Carrion, as this decaying flesh is called, may not sound too tasty to us, but it goes down easily with vultures!

their heads, birds of prey have forward-facing eyes which give them binocular vision. Although this restricts their field of vision in comparison to other birds, the super-sharp focus helps the birds judge distances with amazing accuracy, gaining precise information on the exact location of their prey.

In some species, the birds' eyes are so big that they can hardly move in the sockets – the bird actually has to turn its head to change its field of vision. But from hundreds of feet up in the sky they can pinpoint a creature as tiny as a mouse on the ground and swoop in for the kill.

That's when the bird's other tools come in handy. Large, sharp, curved claws (called talons) are perfectly designed for grabbing on to prey, while hooked, razor-edged bills make light work of tearing off flesh.

THE EAGLE HAS LANDED

Only condors and some vultures are larger than the magnificent eagles. Since Roman times, these birds have been symbols of strength and bravery. Yet they are really quite shy creatures that are keen to avoid danger and happy to keep away from humans. In

GOTCHA!

★ The peregrine falcon is the fastest diver of the lot, and the female is both larger and more aggressive than the male. Thanks to its broad, powerful wings and streamlined body, it can swoop down on its prey at speeds of nearly 200 miles per hour. Now that's what you call fast food!

HAWK EYES ▲

Birds of prey come ready equipped with the right tools for the job of hunting and killing. First and foremost, they have excellent vision. Unlike most birds, which have eyes on the sides of

fact, eagles will only attack when cornered or if their nests are approached.

Golden eagles have long, curved talons which are ideal for picking up a young deer or lamb. These birds are so powerful that they can even carry an animal of their own weight in their fearsome claws, and they never miss a golden opportunity!

WORLDLY WISE

The owl has long been a symbol of wisdom. The ancient Greeks believed it was sacred to Athena, the

goddess of wisdom. In fact many other birds, including blue jays, crows, and grackles, are probably more intelligent.

An owl's major asset is its larger, rounded feathers. At nighttime, these allow the bird to glide silently toward its unsuspecting prey, tuning in to the squeaks of both mice and rats, the staple diet for most kinds of owls. The saucer-shaped ruff of feathers (called the facial disk) around the eyes also helps to reflect sound toward the owl's ears.

ARCTIC A

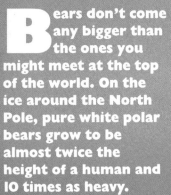

Bears don't come any bigger than the ones you might meet at the top of the world. On the ice around the North Pole, pure white polar bears grow to be almost twice the height of a human and 10 times as heavy.

And though they may look cute and cuddlesome, don't be fooled by appearances –

a polar bear is about as ruthless as the infamous gangster Al Capone!

Making long journeys across deep snow and slippery ice, these polar prowlers are permanently on the lookout for food – birds, fish, plants, and their favorite dish of all, ringed seals. Luckily for them, the expert

hunters have an excellent sense of smell and great strength. A polar bear can knock a seal stone dead with one deft swipe of the paw.

GET OUT OF TOWN!
Churchill is one of Canada's most northerly towns. Each September, its inhabitants play host

to the world's worst tourists – polar bears!

BEAR NECESSITIES
The bears return each year from their summer feeding grounds and break off their journeys to enjoy some snacks from the town's mouth-watering garbage dumps.

LERT

In the wild polar wastelands, survival is the name of the game

Unfortunately for the people of Churchill, some polar bears will pick fights with anyone who gets too close. School children in this town have special classes in bear safety to help keep the visitors at bay.

Aggressive bears are marked with dye to warn folks to keep their distance. The most violent offenders are tranquilized, loaded on to trucks, and driven out of town. And good riddance to bad bears!

SUPERBEAR!

Is there nothing polar bears can't do? Not only are they excellent swimmers, they're surprisingly fast on ice or land. They can run 25 miles per hour, jump over snow hummocks as high as a human being's shoulder, and dive from icebergs into the sea 49 feet below.

Unlike other bears, polar bears have fur on the soles of their paws; this helps them to move over slippery ice. Their powerful claws are so well adapted that they can climb steep walls of ice. They also have an amazing sense of smell, which helps them sniff out seal pups hidden in dens deep beneath the snow, and catch a whiff of food even when it's nearly 10 miles away.

NOW YOU SEE ME...

There's one trick the polar bear has picked up that even the Invisible Man would be proud of. As it sneaks up on its prey, the bear will sometimes cover its black nose with a white paw so that it blends completely into the white background – the ultimate in camouflage!

A STING IN THE TAIL

Bee-ware of nature's striped insects – they've got their own painful weapons!

Upset an insect such as a bee, wasp, or hornet and it may well get its own back – with a painful sting! But for some of these insects, their sting will actually hurt them more than it hurts you. In fact, for most bees, it means certain death.

BEST DEFENSE
Honey bees live together in hives. Different bees have different roles to play. There are thousands of workers (they're the ones you see flying around), hundreds of drones (whose sole job is to mate with the young queens), but just one queen to a hive.

Part of the workers' job is to guard the hive from potential threats such as other bees, bears, and people. Their stings are used as defense weapons. Straight and tiny, they have hooked ends which pull the sting from the bee. But they are vital to the bee's survival. Without it, it soon dies. But even after the sting is detached, its tiny muscles continue to work. These pump poison down the sting and force it deeper into the flesh.

BUMBLING ON
Not all bees die after stinging, though! Bumble bees have long, sharp stings and make a buzzing noise when they fly. They can sting again and again.

In most types of bee sting the poison is produced by glands and causes immediate pain and swelling. If you scrape a sting off your skin right away without squeezing it, the amount of poison it leaves behind should be reduced so the pain won't be so bad.

STRIPE ME DOWN!
There are more than 17,000 kinds of wasps. They have thin waists and, like bees, many of them have distinctive stripes of black and yellow. The stripes can also be black and red or black and white.

Only the female wasp can sting. Unlike most bees, however, she can sting as many times as she likes, without dying. She uses her *ovipositor*, a type of hypodermic needle, which connects to a poison-producing gland. This produces a venom strong enough to paralyze smaller enemies and irritate larger ones.

We call large wasps "hornets." They make paper nests in trees or in the eaves of houses from chewed-up wood and paper fiber. If disturbed, these nervous insects can give a very nasty sting, and their poison produces a swelling that will last for some time.

▲ A beekeeper with a bee-ard – what a close shave!

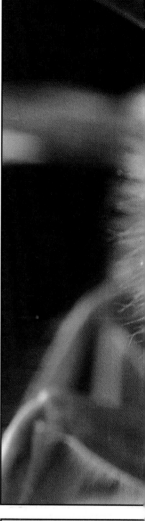

▲ Seen close up, this rear section of a hornet clearly shows its super-sharp, needlelike ovipositor. This is how it injects poison into its potential enemies. Ouch!

▲ *Buzz off! Huge hornets like these can give a nasty sting*

FRIENDS AND FOES

● *Farmers love bumble bees because they pollinate many of the plants needed to feed farm animals.*

● *Wasps called "bee killers" hunt down worker bees, paralyze them, and lay their eggs on them.*

● *Some bugs, called "bee assassins," catch bees in flowers and gobble them up!*

FAKES!

★ Any creature stung by a wasp won't forget what it looked like in a hurry! Other insects that want to protect themselves have developed colored stripes that make them look just like wasps and bees. Enemies can't tell the real thing from the impostors and leave well alone. So let's see how well you would fare!

Can you tell which is the harmless hover fly and which is a real wasp?

A

B

Answer on page 32

If there's one beast in the animal kingdom that's a firm believer in the principle of team work, it must be the majestic lion. These ferocious carnivores are the only species of cats to hunt in groups – and it's the females who do most of the work. Still, the advantages of pooling their resources pay rich dividends at suppertime!

LAZY LAYABOUT LIONS

Working as a group, the lions can take on animals that are much bigger and stronger than themselves. Lions are heavy creatures and unable to run at great speed. But working together, they can bring down a mighty buffalo that may weigh three times as much as each lion. What's

TEAMWORK Lions join forces to hunt down buffalo in Kenya

1 *Females line up to stalk their prey*

more, by pooling their resources, lazy lions use much less energy than they would need if they hunted on their own!

The hunt normally follows a fairly standard pattern. The young and strong females of the pack spread themselves out in a line and begin to stalk their prey.

Meanwhile, the males keep watch to protect the rest of the pride from potential attackers such as hyenas.

QUARRY IN A HURRY

As the females advance on their quarry, the fastest lioness on the flanks will drive some of the prey on the edges of the herd toward the center. A lioness hidden ahead of the herd then picks out a weak or young individual. She kills it by knocking the beast to the ground and biting its neck. This usually takes care of a smaller animal instantly, but it may take several minutes to suffocate a larger creature such as a wildebeest.

Finally, the rest of the pride moves in for feeding. But there's no such thing as a family meal in the lions' world. The hardworking females and their cubs wait patiently for their share of the kill while the bossy males eat their fill.

Mee-ow!

The big cat killer teams that hunt down prey in packs

2 The chase is on. This lioness leaps from her hiding place to pursue an adult African buffalo

3 While the lion holds the buffalo by the hind legs, the female moves in for the kill

DEADLY CARRIERS

Rats and fleas can spread disease. In fact, they make a deadly combination!

There are about 120 different kinds of rats living all over the world. Black rats and brown rats are the best known, but not the best loved! That's not just because of all the damage they cause – destroying crops and killing poultry, lambs, and piglets – but also because of the disease and sickness they spread.

▲ *Houses of plague victims were marked with crosses as a warning*

ONCE BITTEN...

Rats not only eat almost every kind of plant and animal – including other rats – they can also cause fires by gnawing through the insulation around electrical wires. Another serious danger from rats is the fleas they carry. These fleas bite humans and can help to spread dangerous plagues.

STOWAWAYS!

Black and brown rats started life in Asia. These hardy rodents went to Europe via ships or overland, then traveled on to North and South America. When the Crusaders returned to Europe in the 14th century, these sneaky stowaways brought a deadly plague with them – the Black Death.

Between 1334 and 1351, the Black Death caused devastation in countries all over the world, affecting more than a quarter of the population of Europe. The famous plague got its name from the spots of blood which turned black under the skin. The proper name was bubonic plague, which came from the swellings (or buboes) that affected the sufferers.

TINY TERRORS

The Great Plague ravaged London between 1603 and 1665 and, at its height, killed more than 7,000 people in just one week. At this time black rats were a common sight on the dirty, narrow streets of London. When a rat became ill or died, the fleas left their rodent carrier (or host) and sometimes hopped on to humans – bringing with them their deadly disease.

Fleas feed on the blood of living creatures. They get it by puncturing the skin and, in doing this, they spread the dreaded germs. A plague victim's first symptoms would be fever, headache, and pains. Swellings also appeared on the body and then turned into open sores. In a bid to stop the disease from spreading, clothing and possessions were burned. But the plague still managed to wipe out 150,000 people in London alone.

DID YOU KNOW? The earliest recorded plague took place in Athens in 430 B.C.

▲ *Jumping germs: the rat flea in close-up*

SUCKERS!

★ *Malaria is another killer illness passed on by insects. Female anopheles mosquitoes suck human blood after stabbing through the skin with six needle-sharp stylets. As the mosquito sucks up the blood, it injects saliva into its victim to keep the blood flowing freely. That's when the germ that causes malaria enters the bloodstream.*

Up to three million people die of the disease every year, but luckily most cases can now be cured with drugs.

It was once thought that malaria was caused by the nasty atmosphere around marshes. The name comes from the Italian words mal *and* aria, *meaning "bad air."*

The hum of a mosquito is actually the sound of its wings beating about 1,000 times every second.

BLACK OR BROWN?

You can't always tell a black rat (*rattus rattus*, above) from a brown rat (*rattus norvegicus*) just by its color. You also need to compare their sizes and the length of their tails. If the rat is large (weighing just over 1 pound) with a tail that's shorter than its body, it's brown.

Black rats are smaller (about 7 inches, excluding their tails) and weigh about 10 ounces. Despite their name, their fur can be gray-brown or smoky gray as well as black.

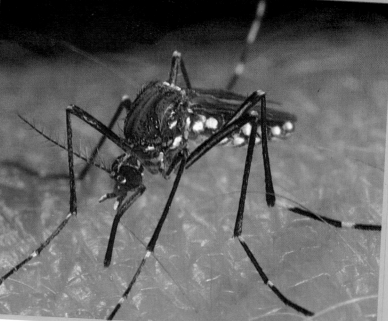

▲ *Sucking up: a hungry mosquito has a snack!*

◄ *Crikey, that's ugly! No it's not ET – it's the wolf spider!*

If the sight of spiders sends you scuttling for a broom, spare a thought for this amazing array of eight-legged horrors. They're lethal!

If you thought spiders were insects, you'd be quite mistaken. Insects have six legs but spiders have eight, which makes them arachnids. There may be as many as 100,000 different kinds of spiders in the world today, and more than 30,000 are already known. And horrible though it may sound, all spiders have fangs and most have poison glands. They use these to capture other animals for food.

If you really are petrified of the critters, here's a reassuring thought. Although a spider's bite can kill insects and other small animals, only a few are dangerous to us humans. Strange, then, that the fear of spiders (or arachnophobia) is so common – especially since most poisonous spiders are only found in very hot countries.

NIFTY MOVERS

Ask any spider-hater what's so creepy about spiders, and you'll get every answer under the sun. But most are in agreement about one point. It's the speedy way the eight-legged arachnids move that really gives them the creeps!

Watch out – the world's deadliest creepy crawlies are about!

ARACHNOPH

FEAR FILE

Scared of spiders? These are the ones to avoid at any cost

THE BLACK WIDOW ▼

The female black widow is the most dangerous spider in North America. Her bite can leave a person paralyzed and in great pain. However, the black widow is far from aggressive – she's really quite a shy, retiring type. Most deaths from her bite have been the result of complications rather than the bite itself, and few victims die as a result.

The black widow earned her name from her ruthless behavior. Sometimes, after mating, the female kills her partner – which isn't difficult as she's four times bigger than him!

TARANTULA

These huge, hairy horrors are the world's largest spiders. The biggest specimens live in the jungles of South America and can measure as much as 10 inches across – and you don't need a ruler to know that's big!

Tarantulas, like other spiders, use powerful juices which dissolve the flesh of their prey. Just by sucking, they can turn a mouse into a small pile of bones and hair in a day and a half.

FUNNEL WEB ▼

Unlike the shy black widow, Australian funnel web spiders can be very hostile and will attack when provoked. A nip from this little demon will result in sweating, sickness, collapse, and possible death. Yikes!

◄SCORPIONS

Like spiders, scorpions are arachnids. They have strong, pincer claws to hold on to their prey and a sharp sting on the end of their tail to kill small animals. Of the 500 or so species, only a few are dangerous to us humans. But don't judge a scorpion by its size – some of the smaller species are the most harmful.

OBIA!

ON YOUR GUARD

Guardian angels or hounds from hell? Are all guard dogs four-legged fiends?

According to Greek mythology, the gates of the underworld were guarded by one of the fiercest creatures ever written about.

Cerberus was a guard dog with a difference – three ferocious heads and a mane of snakes! It took the renowned strongman Hercules to bring the beastly brute under some kind of control.

The legend of Cerberus makes even the meanest of today's watchdogs sound about as nasty as your average pet poodle. Still, faced with the sight of a slavering Rottweiler, would you be prepared to stand your ground in the face of a horrible hound and become a modern day hero like Hercules? No way!

ACTION ALSATIANS

There's nothing new about employing man's best friend as a guardian. For thousands of years, humankind has harnessed dogs' natural instincts to watch over property, possessions, and people.

Dogs have inherited certain traits from their wild relatives, such as wolves and coyotes. They will protect the areas they regard as their own territory and can be trained to frighten off strangers from approaching property, or even to attack anyone foolish enough to ignore those early warning growls.

One of the most common guard dogs is the German shepherd, or Alsatian. First used for herding sheep, this intelligent and responsive dog even looks like a wolf. All over the world, police forces train Alsatians to help them track down criminals, and their fierce barking can help control large crowds of people. But Alsatians aren't only famous for being fearsome – they make great guide dogs, too, and are handy at leading blind owners through busy streets.

THE BIG ONE

The Rottweiler is probably the best known of all the big guard dogs. Big and beefy, these mighty mean-looking mutts are descended from the camp dogs that followed Roman armies almost 2,000 years ago.

The Romans used them for herding cattle and sheep. But it wasn't until the 19th century that the modern Rottweiler was developed in the German town of – guess what?– Rottweil! They're fiercely protective and territorial by nature, which makes them ideal guard dogs. But perhaps they're best known for being BIG – some adult Rottweilers are more than 2 feet in height and weigh a massive 110 pounds.

▲ Grrr, would you pick a row with a mean-looking Rottweiler?!

WHAT A HOWLER!

It's not surprising that dogs make such good guards. Like their distant relative, the wolf, they're territorial by nature.

All sorts of myths exist about the wolf, but one of the saddest must be that these wild creatures often attack people. This has led to the mass destruction of wolves in several parts of the world.

In fact, wolves avoid people as much as possible. The howls that they use to communicate may sound scary to us but it's the caribou, deer, elk, and moose in the area that should be really scared – they're the ones the wolves want!

What BIG teeth you have...

★ No wonder we think of wolves as being wild, hungry human-hunters. From early childhood, we're told fairy tales featuring big, bad wolves who are out to gobble up children and little piggies at the drop of a hat!

▲ Hoodwinked... Red Riding Hood meets the Wolf Man!

▲ Go get him! Alsatians are a police officer's best friend

It may look like a piece of dead wood floating in the water, but when a crocodile opens its mouth, the difference between this giant reptile and a log soon becomes clear. No piece of wood could snap your leg off with just one bite.

Crocodiles live near rivers, swamps, and marshes in tropical countries. Webbed feet allow them to walk on soft ground, and their long tails can power them through the water. But watch out – crocodiles have one sneaky trick that makes them almost invisible to their prey. They float along with just their eyes and nostrils sticking out above the surface. Then, at the vital moment of attack, a valve in the crocodile's throat keeps water out while those cavernous jaws open wide...

COME ON IN

Inside the mouth of a crocodile is probably not everyone's idea of a fun place to be. But two kinds of animal do venture inside the croc's mouth with no dire consequences.

Freshly hatched baby crocs are carried to the river in their mothers' jaws. And plucky plover birds pick food out from between the teeth of crocodiles – these living toothbrushes act as their very own daring dentists!

DROWN THE HATCH!

Crocodiles and alligators spend most of their lives in water. They're not keen on leaving their natural environment in search of food. However, should a pig, dog, antelope, or even a cow stray too near the water's edge, these wily old warriors (which can live for up to 60 years) will pounce with surprising agility.

Crocodiles and alligators have their own special way of making a meal of their prey. Lying in wait, they'll drag their chosen victim underwater, knocking it over with a blow from the head or tail. Underwater, the victim soon drowns, leaving the croc with phase two of its meal.

MY TOOTH HATH COME LOOTHE!

Crocodiles and alligators have their own special way of devouring their large meals (including people) – they reduce them to convenient, bite-size pieces!

Alligators have about 100 teeth, but when it comes to cutting through flesh or chewing, they're not quite the right shape! Seizing their prey in their massive jaws, the powerful creatures spin their dinner violently in the water, twisting off chunks of flesh which are much easier to swallow. These voracious hunters often lose teeth in the struggle but, as with sharks, new ones quickly grow through to fill in the gaps. Maybe that's why crocodiles always look as though they're smiling...

FAMILY TIES
Crocs and alligators are descended from a large and ancient group of reptiles. Fossils show that their ancestors reached lengths of 45 feet – that's nearly as long as two city buses!

▲ *Say cheese! The unmistakable smile of the crocodile*

SPOT THE

When you're staring into the jaws of what you think is a crocodile (but could well be an alligator) here are some tips on how to identify your aggressor!

ON THE CROC!

▲ Snap attack! A Nile crocodile homes in on lunch with a herd of zebra

DIFFERENCE

1 Are you being attacked? If you are, then it's more likely to be a crocodile – alligators are much less aggressive.

2 Does it have a long, rounded snout? If it does, then it sounds like an alligator. Most crocodiles have a snout that comes to a point at the front.

3 When the beast has its mouth shut, can you see a long tooth sticking up from the lower jaw? If you can, it's definitely a croc!

▲ Round and a snout – the American alligator

MISSING LIN

Strange as it may seem, a glowing ball of gases about 93 million miles above us, and a mass 332,000 times greater than Earth, is the ultimate source of all food.

The sun provides energy in the form of heat and light. Plants convert this into their own food, releasing oxygen into the atmosphere as a result. Some of the sun's energy is passed on to animals, which eat the plants. Those animals will, in turn, provide food and energy for creatures that prey on them. This system of interdependence between animals and plants is called a *food chain*.

The food chain does not end when an animal dies. The decaying bodies of dead animals contain substances that help plants to grow. Bacteria break down the bodies and help the nourishing elements enrich the soil.

THE CHAIN GAME

In any forest, ocean, or desert there will be many different kinds of plants and animals feeding on each other (and even, in some cases, on themselves!). There will be many food chains overlapping and interlocking, giving the impression of a complex "food web." These complicated patterns of who-eats-who and who-eats-what are delicately balanced. Environmental influences such as pollution can affect the whole chain and play havoc with the balance.

The sun provides energy for plants

Birds such as falcons catch and eat the fish

Plankton grows in water using sunlight and minerals

Small fish in the river eat the plankton

Larger fish eat the smaller fish

It's not just a dog-eat-dog world out there! Our food chain shows how animals rely on each other for survival

Trees use sunlight to make food. They bear fruit, seeds, and nuts

Squirrels feed on nuts and seeds

Humans sow crops such as wheat and corn

Small animals such as mice and voles eat the crops

Foxes eat small animals such as birds, rabbits, mice, and rats

Plant and animal remains enrich the soil

INDEX

ANSWERS TO QUICK QUIZ QUESTIONS

Page 11 c) 300 times. **Page 14** The eagle. **Page 19** A) is the real wasp.